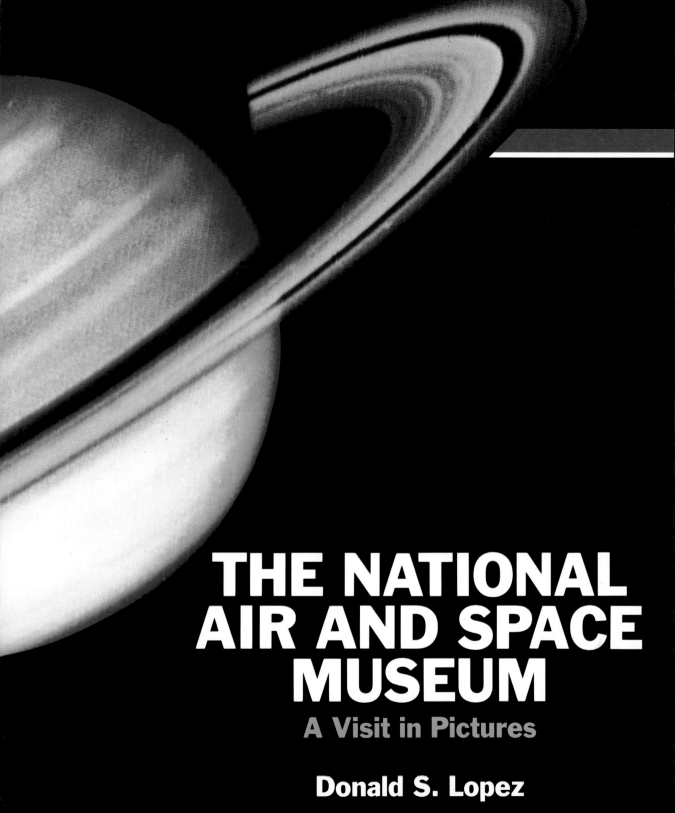

THE NATIONAL AIR AND SPACE MUSEUM

A Visit in Pictures

Donald S. Lopez

Smithsonian Institution Press, Washington, D.C.

Robert Taylor - 86 -

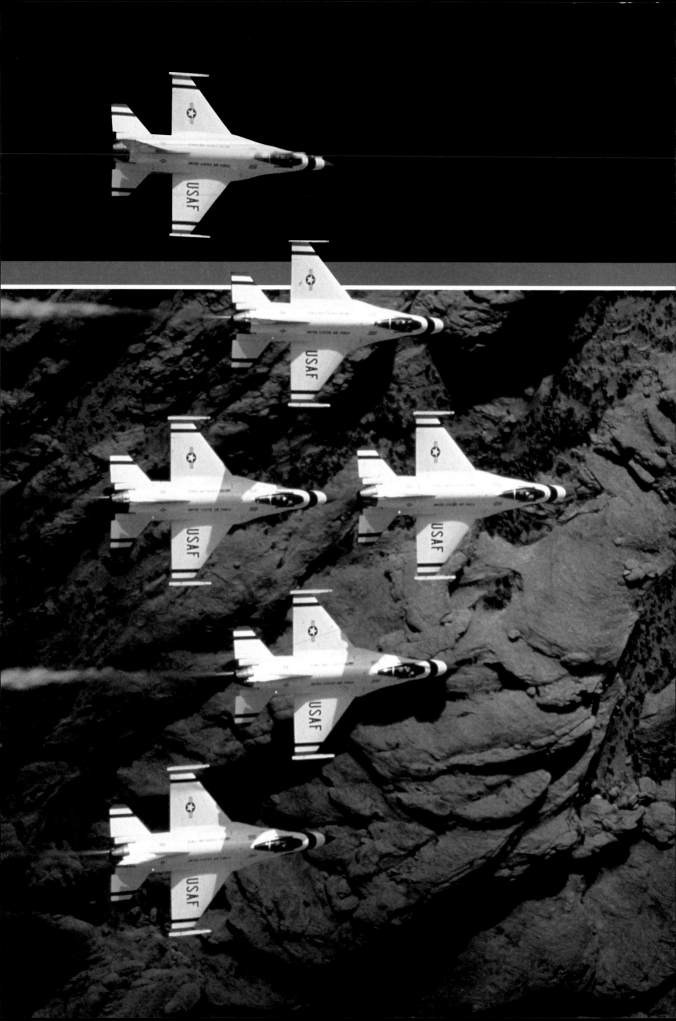

INTRODUCTION

In these pages unfolds a visual celebration of mankind's remarkable air and space achievements during the twentieth century. Since its opening on Bicentennial Day in 1976, this awe-inspiring building has become host to nearly ten million visitors annually and is the most heavily attended museum in the world.

One reason for this extraordinary popularity is that all of the aircraft and, where possible, all the spacecraft are the real thing—not just models or replicas. Spacecraft that remain on the Moon, in orbit on another planet, or that have been destroyed during reentry are represented by other actual spacecraft that were never launched or by engineering prototypes. Another great attraction for aviation buffs is the Paul E. Garber Facility in nearby Maryland where more than one hundred additional aircraft are exhibited. Housed there are the B-29 *Enola Gay* and many rare German and Japanese fighters and bombers of World War II.

Established by congressional action in 1946 as the National Air Museum, what is now known as The National Air and Space Museum (NASM) occupied temporary and inadequate quarters for more than a quarter century. It is hard to imagine the row of rockets and one long tin shed in what is now the Enid A. Haupt Garden next to the Smithsonian Castle.

So the museum itself has progressed, as have the technologies that bring us to the final decade of the century. The nine pictorial sections of this book are arranged by museum gallery or by significant periods of aerospace history:

> Milestones of Flight
> Early Flight
> World War I
> Golden Age of Flight
> Air Transport
> World War II
> Jet Age
> Space Age
> Paul E. Garber Facility

We hope that this picture visit will serve as a pleasant reminder of your trip to the National Air and Space Museum—or as an invitation to come and see its riches for yourself.

Photographs on pages 1–8:

Page 1: A reproduction Wright Glider flies over the Kitty Hawk dunes in this scene from the IMAX film *On the Wing*. **Pages 2–3:** A fisheye lens view of the Milestones of Flight gallery. **Pages 4–5:** As a result of the Voyager planetary probe, scientists learned that the rings of the planet Saturn are made up of thousands of small bands. **Pages 6–7:** Royal Air Force Avro Lancasters are depicted landing at an airfield in England in the painting *Last Flight Home* by Robert Taylor.

Left: Six General Dynamics F-16s of the United States Air Force Thunderbirds fly in formation over Nevada.

MILESTONES
OF
FLIGHT

N-X-211

A striking feature about the air- and spacecraft in this gallery is the relatively short time between enormous advances in mastery of Earth's atmosphere and beyond.

Here two of the great icons of air and space history are separated by a mere 20 feet in placement and less than 66 years in time. Yet the Wright Flyer, in 1903, could fly only 852 feet while the Apollo ll, in 1969, traveled some 240,000 miles to the Moon and back. Lindbergh's *Spirit of St. Louis*, conqueror of the Atlantic in 1927, is suspended only a short distance from an engineering prototype of the Pioneer 10 planetary probe that left the solar system in 1986.

Considering that no one could have imagined the aviation milestones ahead when the Wright brothers launched their first hesitant biplane in 1903, it is interesting to speculate what scientific and technological advances the next 85 years will bring.

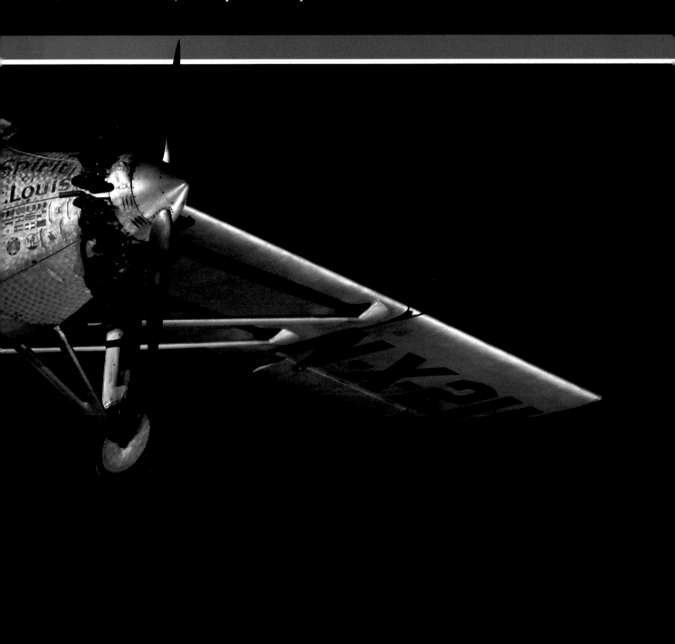

Preceding page: On May 20 and 21, 1927, the 25-year-old Charles Lindbergh made the first solo flight across the Atlantic in the Ryan NYP, *Spirit of St. Louis*. Lindbergh flew from New York to Paris in 33½ hours.

1 The flags on the nose of the *Spirit of St. Louis* represent the countries Lindbergh visited on his tour of 1927 and 1928. **2** On December 17, 1903, on the dunes near Kitty Hawk, North Carolina, the Wright Flyer, piloted by Orville Wright, made the first successful airplane

1

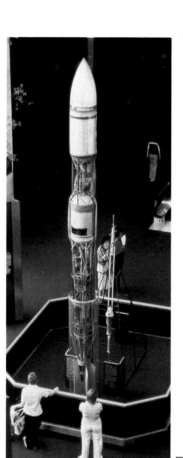

2

3

6

4

5

flight. **3** Mannequin of Orville Wright in the prone pilot position on the lower wing of the Wright Flyer. **4** Two of rocket pioneer Dr. Robert H. Goddard's early rockets: the smaller, the world's first successful liquid-propellant rocket, flew on March 16, 1926; the larger rocket flew in 1941. **5** The North American X-15 rocket-powered research plane paved the way for America's entry into space, reaching a speed of 4500 mph and an altitude of 67 miles. **6** Captain Charles "Chuck" Yeager became the first to exceed the speed of sound in this Bell X-1 on October 14, 1947. **7** Wiley Post twice flew the Lockheed Vega *Winnie Mae* around the world, with Harold Gatty in 1931 and solo in 1933. **8** Astronaut Ed White became the first American to "walk" in space when he climbed out of this Gemini 4 capsule while in orbit on June 3, 1965. **9** On February 20, 1962, John Glenn became the first American to orbit the Earth with his three-orbit flight in the Mercury capsule, *Friendship Seven*. **10** A child explores the heat shield of the *Friendship Seven*. (Photo by Susan Jenkins Shawhan)

7

8

9

10

13

11 A docent describes the Apollo 11 Command Module to a tour group. **12** In July 1969 this Apollo 11 Command Module carried astronauts Armstrong, Aldrin, and Collins to lunar orbit and back to Earth. Collins remained in orbit while Armstrong and Aldrin landed on the moon on July 20. **13** A young visitor touches a piece of the Moon. **14** Visitors inspect the Viking

Mars lander on the simulated surface of Mars. **15** Visitors surround the Apollo 11 Command Module on the tenth anniversary of the first Moon landing. **16** The Mariner 2 planetary probe became the first probe to successfully survey another planet when, on December 14, 1962, it approached within some 20,000 miles of Venus. **17** Viking Mars landers made soft landings on Mars on July 20 and September 3, 1976. While much valuable data was gathered, there were no signs of life on Mars. **18** On November 20, 1953, this Douglas D-558-2 Sky-rocket, piloted by NASA test pilot Scott Crossfield, became the first airplane to reach Mach 2, twice the speed of sound. **19** Father and son view the Milestones of Flight gallery. (Photo by Rae Hart)

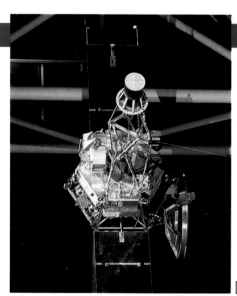

16

17

18

19

EARLY FLIGHT

It is coincidental that two of the most important advances in the history of flight sprang from the minds of brothers. In 1783 Joseph and Etienne Montgolfier of France designed and built the hot air balloon that carried man aloft for the first time, launching the science of aerostation, or lighter than air flight. In the United States 120 years later, Orville and Wilbur Wright designed, built, and flew the first successful powered airplane. None of the brothers were trained as scientists or

engineers, yet by careful and methodical experimentation they solved the basic problems of flight within the atmosphere. Improvement followed improvement as other experimenters contributed to the modern science of flight. Altitude, speed, and distance records were set and broken with regularity. International air races for the Gordon Bennett Cup and the Schneider Trophy caught the fancy of the public, making popular heroes of dare-

devil pilots. Reconnaissance and bombing were tested, and beginning with World War I the airplane changed the course of modern warfare.

1

MONTGOLFIER IN THE CLOUDS

CONSTRUCTING OF AIR BALLOONS FOR THE GRAND MONARQUE

2

1 Model of the Montgolfier balloon that, on November 21, 1783, carried the first humans to fly, French noblemen Pilâtre de Rozier and the Marquis d'Arlandes, into the air over Versailles. **2** A British print lampooning Montgolfier's boast that he could conquer Gibraltar with his balloons. (Photo by Ed Castle) **3** Model of the Charles balloon in which Professor Charles and his assistant M. N. Robert made the first ascent in a hydrogen balloon. Their two-hour flight was witnessed by some 200,000 Parisians. **4** The Wright Military Flyer was purchased by the United States Army in 1909 after trials at Fort Myer, Virginia. It was the first airplane purchased by any government.

3

4

5 Closeup of the pilot's position in the 1912 Glenn Curtiss Headless Pusher. The ailerons were controlled by the pilot leaning to one side or the other. **6** This Curtiss Headless Pusher was used extensively in barnstorming and air exhibitions. It was called headless because the forward control surfaces typical of earlier models had been removed. **7** Calbraith Rodgers attempted to fly this Wright EX *Vin Fiz* across the United States within thirty days in quest of a

5

6

$50,000 prize. The flight took him forty-nine days; nevertheless it was the first transcontinental flight. **8** This Blériot XI is an advanced version of the one that made the first flight across the English Channel on July 25, 1909, piloted by its designer, Louis Blériot.

7

8

WORLD WAR I

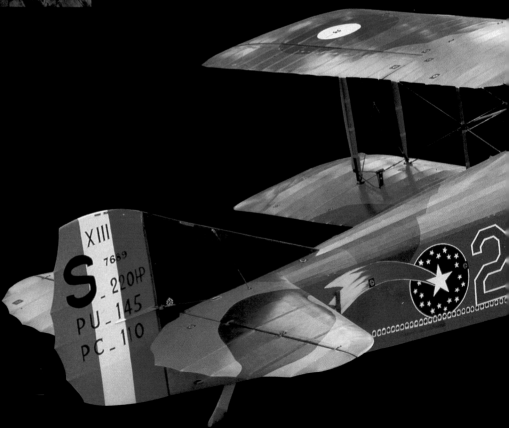

It is unfortunate but true that technology advances at a rapid rate during prolonged periods of warfare. This was the case especially in the field of aviation during World War I, or the Great War as it was then known. When war broke out in August of 1914, airplanes were flimsy, fragile machines with limited speed, range, and altitude capabilities; their only military value was thought to be in the reconnaissance role, formerly the duty of the cavalry. Throughout the war new and better airframes, armament, and engines were developed. By the end of the war in November 1918, both the Allies and Central Powers had thousands of combat airplanes, many capable of flying above 20,000 feet for hundreds of miles and at speeds of more than 100 mph. The horrors of the stalemated war in the trenches turned the attention of the public to the "knights of the air." Fighting high above the muddy battlefield, air aces soon became the heroes of the day.

Preceding page: The sturdy French Spad XIII was widely used by the Allies in World War I.
Inset: Howard Chandler Christy portrait of Captain Eddie Rickenbacker, America's leading ace of World War I. Rickenbacker scored most of his twenty-six victories in a Spad.

1

2

3

1 The Albatros D.Va was the last in the series of Albatros fighters that were the mainstay of the German Air Force in World War I. Baron von Richthofen scored sixty of his eighty victories in the Albatros. **2** The terms of the Armistice specifically called for all Fokker D.VIIs, one of the best fighters of World War I, to be turned over to the Allies. **3** This SPAD XIII, in the markings of the 22nd Aero Squadron, was flown by six-victory ace Captain Arthur Raymond Brooks. (Photo by Ross Chapple) **4** This painting by John F. Amendola, Jr., depicts de Havilland DH-4s in test flights at McCook Field, Dayton, Ohio. **5** A typical World War I Air Service recruiting poster. (Photo by Ed Castle) **6** The de Havilland DH-4 was used both for aerial reconnaissance and for bombing by the British and Americans in World War I. Manufactured under license from the British, it was the only American-built airplane to see action in the war.

4

JOIN THE
AIR SERVICE
and
SERVE
in
FRANCE

DO IT
NOW

5

6

GOLDEN AGE OF FLIGHT

The years between the two world wars are generally referred to as the Golden Age of Flight, but it is unlikely they were considered golden by the struggling pilots, designers, and manufacturers of the late teens and early twenties. With the success of Charles Lindbergh's epic transatlantic flight of 1927 came astonishing progress. Advances in airframe design and the development of the first highly reliable air-cooled engine, the Wright Whirlwind, prepared the aviation industry for the

surge of interest in flying that Lindbergh generated.

The following twelve years saw remarkable improvements in airplane performance and reliability. New records in altitude, endurance, and speed were set with astonishing regularity. The names of the pilots—Jimmy Doolittle, Roscoe Turner, Frank Hawks, Amelia Earhart, Jacqueline Cochran—and their airplanes—Gee Bee, Wedell-Williams, Travel Air, Lockheed Vega, and Northrop Gamma—

became popular household words. More important than their headline-making exploits, however, was a wealth of technological advances that pointed to an even more ambitious future.

Preceding page: On May 2, 1923, United States Army Air Service Lieutenants Kelly and Macready landed the Fokker T-2 in San Diego after 26 hours and 50 minutes in the air, completing the first nonstop transcontinental flight.

1 Amelia Earhart became the first woman to make a nonstop solo flight across the Atlantic when she landed her Lockheed Vega in Londonderry, Northern Ireland, on May 21, 1932. **2** On October 25, 1925, Lieutenant Jimmy Doolittle won the prestigious Schneider Trophy Race for the United States in this Curtiss R3C-2, with an average speed of 232.57 mph. **3** Charles and Anne Lindbergh explored flight routes across the Pacific in 1931 and the North and South Atlantic in 1933 in

[2]

[1]

[3]

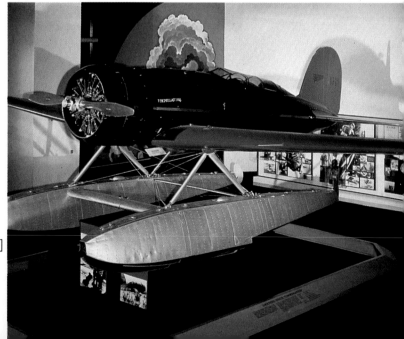

their Lockheed Sirius *Tingmissartoq*. **4** Howard Hughes set a world speed record of 352.322 mph on September 13, 1935, in his Hughes H-1 racer. In a nonstop flight on January 19, 1937, he set a transcontinental record of 7 hours and 28 minutes in the same airplane. **5** Brothers Fred and Algene Key took off from Meridian, Mississippi, in their Curtis Robin J-1 *Ole Miss* on June 4, 1935. They remained aloft for twenty-seven days, setting a world record for sustained flight. **6** The Lindbergh's Lock-

heed Sirius *Tingmissartoq* is shown on the ramp prior to launching in John Paul Jones's painting *Preparing for Atlantic Survey.*

4

5

6

7 The all-metal Boeing P-26A *Peashooter* was the first monoplane fighter and the last open cockpit fighter accepted by the United States Army Air Corps. **8** In the 1930s the Boeing F4B-4 was flown by the Navy and Marines and, as the P-12E, by the Army Air Corps. **9** Major Al Williams used this Grumman G-22 *Gulfhawk II* as a flying laboratory for the Gulf Oil Company and to demonstrate precision flying and aerobatics. **10** The 804-foot-long Zeppelin *Hindenburg* was the pride of Hitler's Germany

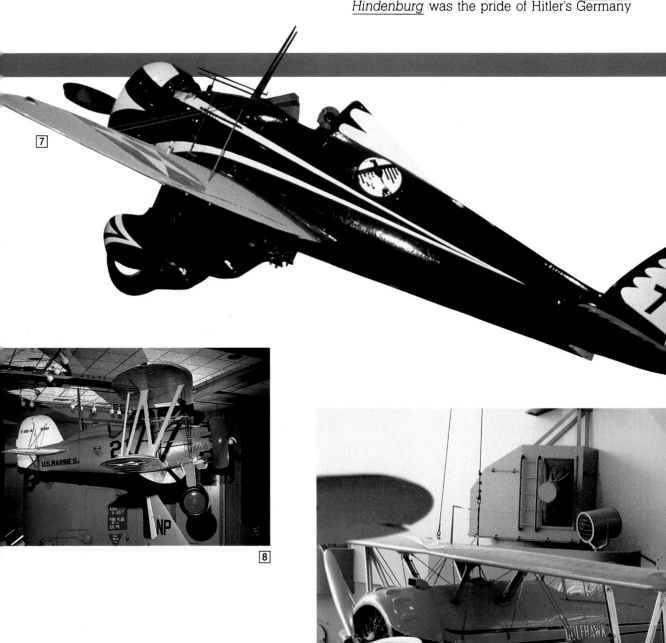

until it was destroyed in a spectacular hydrogen explosion at Lakehurst, New Jersey, in 1937. (Photo by Ed Castle) **11** Steve Wittman's *Buster* was one of the most successful racing planes of the post World War II period. **12** The Curtiss F9C-2 Sparrowhawk, was launched and recovered in flight, from the United States Navy airships, *Akron* and *Macon*. **13** The Beech *Staggerwing* was one of the best performing and most popular business aircraft of the Golden Age.

IN 2 DAYS TO NORTH AMERICA!
DEUTSCHE ZEPPELIN-REEDEREI

10

11

12

13

Air transport as we know it today had its beginnings in the years immediately following World War I. Wartime improvements in aircraft performance had first made practical the regular transport of passengers, mail, and cargo by air. While the United States concentrated primarily on the movement of mail, Germany, France, and England established regularly scheduled passenger airlines shortly after the war. On both sides of the Atlantic an abundance of surplus military airplanes, as well as trained pilots to fly them, encouraged the sudden growth of a new industry.

In 1929 the first transcontinental airline service began in the United States. A combination carrier service—train by night and plane by day—sped passengers from coast to coast in just 48 hours. In the 1950s jet-powered airplanes came into use, making it possible for today's jumbo jets to cross the United States in roughly five hours.

Preceding page: On April 17, 1926, Western Air Service Inc. began mail and passenger operations between Salt Lake City and Los Angeles, flying Liberty-powered Douglas M-2s. **Inset:** A colorful Air Mail stamp of the 1920s. (Photo by Ed Castle)

1 This fullscale diorama depicts mail being loaded in a <u>Western Air Service Douglas M-2</u>. **2** The <u>Pitcairn PA-5 Mailwing</u>, designed as a mailplane, began service on the New York to Atlanta run with Pitcairn Air Service, a forerunner of Eastern Air Lines. **3** The sleek <u>Northrop Alpha</u> was used to fly light perishables such as strawberries and orchids from coast to coast. **4** The rugged <u>Ford Tri-motor 5-AT</u>, a sixteen-passenger transport, was first produced in 1928 by the Ford Motor Company. The Ford name helped instill confidence in the safety of air transport. **5** The <u>Boeing 247D</u>, which entered service in 1933, was the first of the modern airliners.

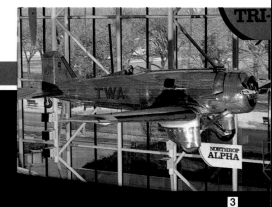

3

4

5

6

7

8

6 The Douglas DC-3, which entered service in 1936, revolutionized the commercial airline industry. By 1938, 95 percent of United States airline traffic was on DC-3s. **7** Passengers are shown boarding a Pan American Boeing 314 Clipper in San Francisco harbor in Robert Taylor's painting *Limitless Horizons.* **8** This Federal Express Falcon 20 was the first aircraft of the soon-burgeoning air express industry. **9** Visitors inspect the engine exhibit in the Air Transportation gallery. **10** Viewed from the balcony above, the gallery provides a panorama of air transport history. (Photo by Mike Mitchell) **11** Visitors enter the nose section of a Douglas DC-7C, one of the last transcontinental propeller-driven transports.

9

10

11

WORLD WAR II

As in the first world war, aviation technology advanced at a rapid pace during World War II. Mass production led to the manufacture of hundreds of thousands of aircraft and innovative training techniques helped prepare the aircrews to operate them. Radar and jet propulsion, although invented before the out-

break of the war, became operational during this period.

Airpower played a pivotal role in World War II. A deciding factor in many major battles, aircraft exerted a force in all combat arenas. The Battle of Britain, the first battle to be fought entirely in the air, was won by Britain's Royal Air Force with the help of the newly developed radar warning system. The great

Pacific sea battles were fought almost exclusively by carrier-based aircraft launched against enemy fleets and ground installations. The course of the Pacific war was reversed in June 1942 when United States Navy aircraft destroyed four Japanese fleet carriers in the Battle of Midway.

Preceding page: The Messerschmitt Bf 109G was the mainstay of the German Luftwaffe fighter force. More than 21,000 were produced.

1

2

3

Spitfire MK. VII

1 Cockpit of the Messerschmitt Bf 109G after restoration. **2** Arguably the best fighter of World War II, the North American P-51D Mustang combined speed, handling, and firepower with exceptional range. **3** The Supermarine Spitfire Mark 7 is a high altitude variant of the famous Spitfire line used by the Royal Air Force throughout World War II. **4** The Grumman F4F-4 Wildcat was the United States Navy's principal fighter for the first two years of World War II. **5** A Curtiss P-40E, in the markings made famous by the Flying Tigers, is suspended above a United States Marine F4U-1D Corsair. **6** The range, firepower, and remarkable maneuverability of the Mitsubishi Zero surprised the Allies when first encountered in World War II. This model is the A6M5.

4

5

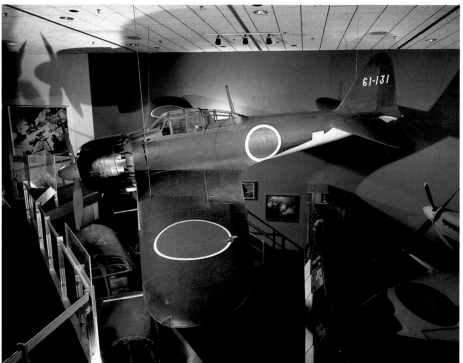

6

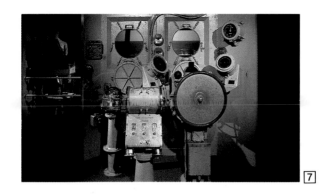

7 The navigation bridge of a World War II U.S. aircraft carrier is reproduced in the Sea-Air Operations gallery. The bridge is a great favorite with young visitors. **8** One of the best Italian fighters of World War II, the Macchi C.202 Folgore (Lightning) wears the markings of one of Italy's crack fighter squadrons, the 4° Stormo. (Photo by Mike Mitchell) **9** The Douglas SBD Dauntless dive bomber won immortality for its major role in sinking four Japanese carriers

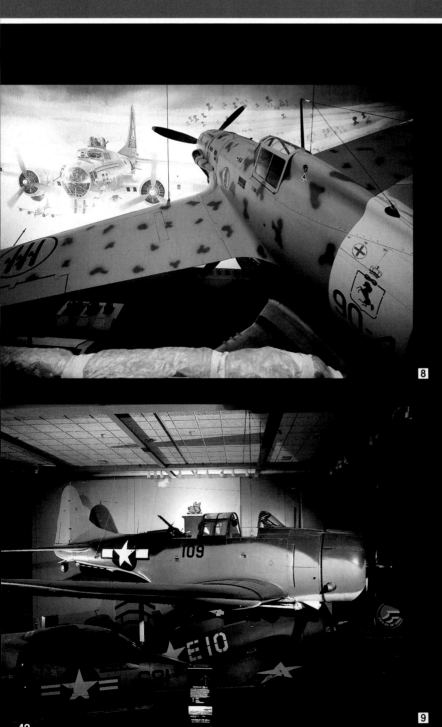

during the Battle of Midway, the turning point in the Pacific war. **10** The Sikorsky XR-4 helicopter made the first extended crosscountry flight by a helicopter in the United States. R-4s saw limited action in Burma and Great Britain late in World War II. **11** In the painting *Into the Teeth of the Tiger* by William S. Phillips, a Curtiss P-40 has just collided with a Nakajima Ki.43 Oscar over China. **12** Closeup of the shark mouth design used on the Curtiss P-40 by the Flying Tigers in China. **13** Keith Ferris's 25-by-75 foot mural, *Fortresses under Fire*, dominates the World War II Aviation gallery. It depicts an actual combat mission over Wiesbaden, Germany, in August 1944.

JET AGE

Sir Frank Whittle, as a young Royal Air Force cadet and officer, originated the basic concept of the jet engine and obtained a patent in 1931. By 1937 he had successfully ground tested the engine, but flight testing of his design had to wait until 1941. The first flight of a jet-propelled airplane took place in Germany on August 27, 1939, when the Heinkel He 178 lifted off the runway. It was powered by a Heinkel jet engine designed by the young

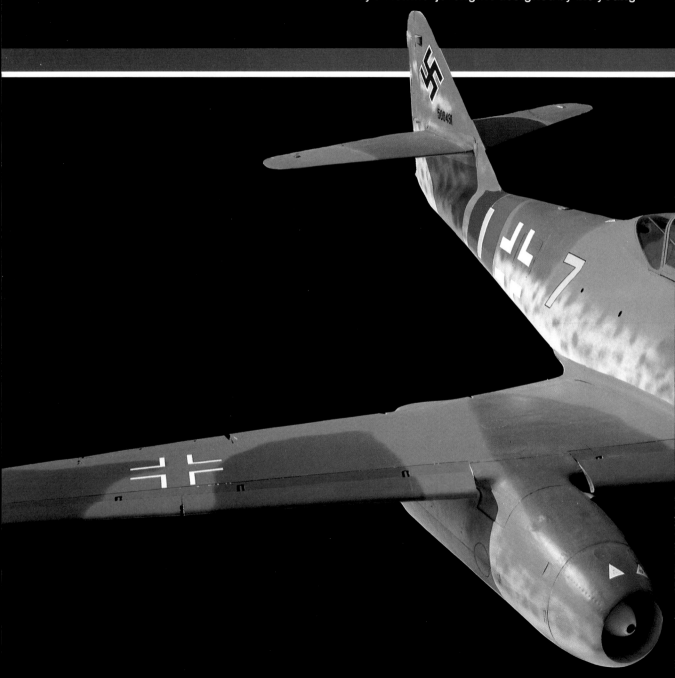

German scientist Hans von Ohain. By late 1944 the German Messerschmitt Me 262 and the British Gloster Meteor were operational.

Another major breakthrough occurred on October 14, 1947, when Captain Chuck Yeager became the first to exceed the speed of sound in the Bell X-1 *Glamorous Glennis*, thus opening up a whole new realm of flight.

The first jet airliner, the de Havilland Comet, entered commercial service in 1952, but two disastrous crashes curtailed its use. In 1958 the Boeing 707 began transatlantic service, cutting the time between the United States and Europe almost in half. Today it is possible to jet across the Atlantic in the Anglo-French Concorde at speeds in excess of Mach 2 in a mere three-and-one-half hours.

Preceding page: The Messerschmitt Me 262 Schwalbe (Swallow) was the first jet to become operational. Powered by two Junkers Jumo engines it was more than 100 mph faster than the fastest Allied fighter.

1 The V/STOL Hawker Siddeley XV-6A Kestrel was the forerunner of the Harrier used by the British in the Falkland war and by the United States Marines as the AV-8. **2** The Lockheed XP-80 *Lulubelle*, designed and built in only 143 days, was first flown on January 8, 1944. This very successful design became the first operational United States jet fighter. **3** The Mach 2 Lockheed F-104 Starfighter was called "the missile with the man in it" because of its extremely

1

2

3

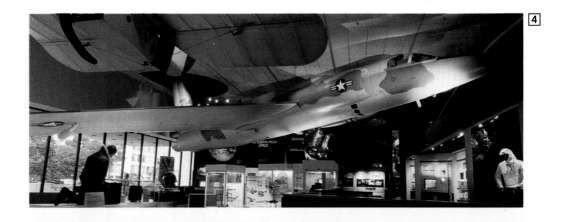

4

small wings. This aircraft was used by the National Aeronautics and Space Administration as a flying testbed and a chase plane. **4** The Lockheed U-2 high altitude reconnaissance plane was designed and built in great secrecy in Lockheed designer Kelly Johnson's "Skunk Works." **5** In 1954 the Boeing 367-80, one of the most important aircraft in aviation history, first flew. Its design inspired both the 707 that revolutionized air transport and the United States Air Force tanker, the KC-135. **6** The Douglas A-4 Skyhawk, one of the most versatile and effective Navy attack aircraft, is known as *Heinemann's Hotrod* after its designer Ed Heinemann.

5

6

7 Visitors enter the Jet Aviation gallery through the nacelle of a Boeing 747 engine. **8** This 1/100 scale model of the nuclear-powered aircraft carrier *Enterprise* took the builder, Steve Henninger, twelve years to complete. (Photo by Perry Greza) **9** The Sea-Air Operations gallery was formally commissioned CM-76, the *U.S.S. Smithsonian*, by Secretary of the Navy Middendorf. **10** In flight the Lockheed U-2 resem-

7

8

bles a high-performance sailplane. **11** Royal
Jordanian Air Force Hawker Hunters are shown
over Jordan in the painting *Hunters of Wadi
Rum* by William S. Phillips.

9

10

11

SPACE AGE

Following World War II many scientific instruments were launched into the lower reaches of space by rockets based on the German V-2 ballistic missile used against England in the war. The space age really began, however, on October 4, 1957, when the Soviets launched the first earth satellite, *Sputnik 1*, into orbit. The space race was on and a few months later, on January 31, 1958, the first United States satellite, *Explorer 1*, was orbited. In 1961 Soviet cosmonaut Yuri

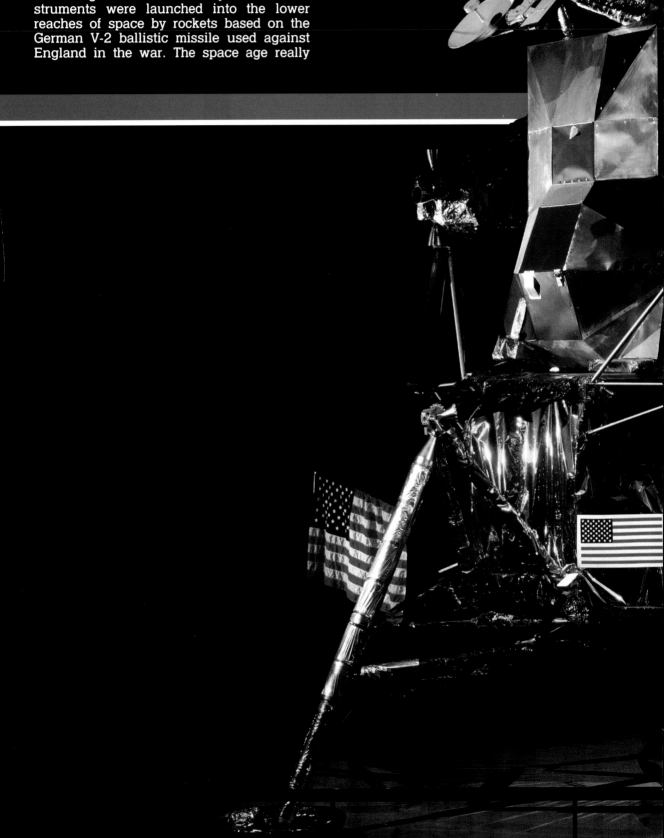

Gagarin became the first man to orbit the earth; the following year astronaut John Glenn became the first American to do so.

In July 1969 the United States met the goal established by President Kennedy when Apollo 11 astronauts Neil Armstrong and Buzz Aldrin landed on the moon and returned safely to earth. Five more pairs of Americans would land on the moon by the end of the Apollo program.

Today planetary probes explore the solar system and outer space is virtually cluttered with satellites. These unmanned spacecraft send back invaluable data on the weather, transmit communication signals around the world, provide agricultural and geological data, and perform a myriad of tasks that would have been impossible before the space age.

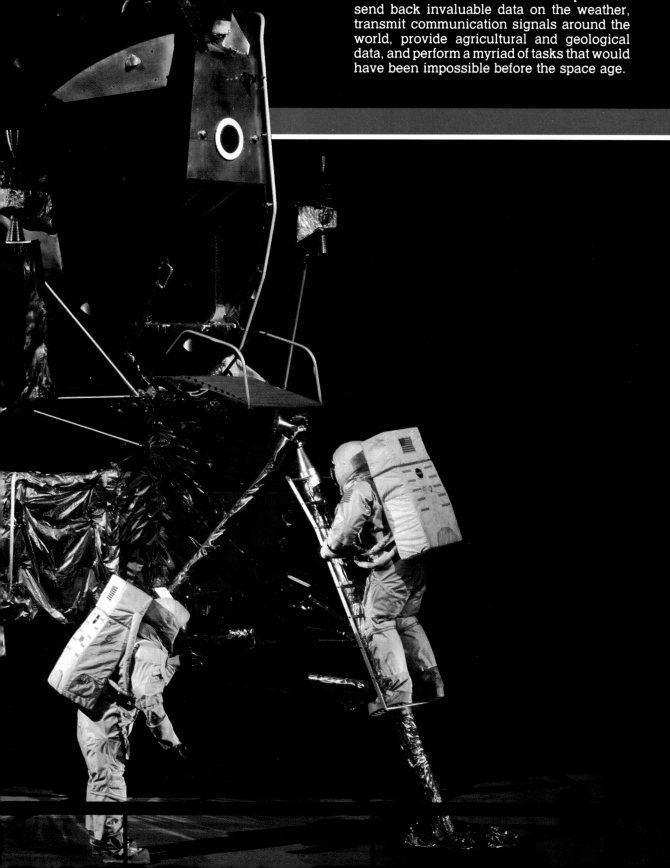

1

Preceding page: The Lunar Module transported two astronauts from lunar orbit to the lunar surface and back. The bottom section of the module remained on the Moon.

1 The space age began on October 4, 1957, when the Soviet Union placed the first artificial satellite, Sputnik 1, into orbit around Earth. **2** The United States entered the space age when the Explorer 1 satellite was lifted into orbit on January 31, 1958, by a Jupiter C rocket. **3** Mockup of the

2

3

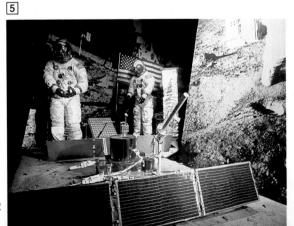

4

5

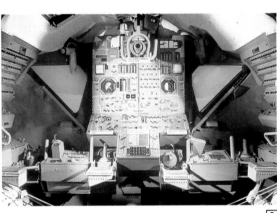

6

52

Lunar Module cockpit; two astronauts controlled the module from a standing position. **4** Precursor of the powerful launch vehicles of the space age, the V-2 missile was used by the Germans against England in World War II. **5** This diorama, featuring actual mission spacesuits, depicts astronauts Armstrong and Aldrin on the lunar surface on July 20, 1969. **6** The Lunar Rover is a two-seat electric-powered vehicle that transported astronauts on the surface of the Moon on Apollo 15, 16, and 17. Three Lunar Rovers remain on the Moon. **7** Five F-1 engines powered the first stage of the Saturn V launch vehicle used on all the lunar-landing missions. Each of these kerosene and liquid oxygen fueled engines generated 1,600,000 pounds of thrust. **8** Mannequin with food container in the wardroom of the Skylab Orbital Workshop. Launched on May 26, 1973, Skylab was the first United States space station.

[7]

[8]

9

10

9 Astronauts Hartsfield and Coates in the cockpit of the Shuttle Orbiter *Discovery* in a scene from the IMAX film, *The Dream Is Alive*. **10** The Space Shuttle, powered by its three main engines and two solid rocket boosters, leaves the launch pad. **11** Astronauts Nelson and van Hoften repair the disabled satellite Solar Max in the cargo bay of the Shuttle Orbiter *Challenger* in a scene from the IMAX film, *The Dream Is Alive*. **12** Space-suited mannequin in the upper section of the Skylab Orbital Workshop, a modified S-IVB stage of the Saturn V launch vehicle. **13** A Space Shuttle Orbiter is transported from California to Florida atop a specially modified Boeing 747.

11

12

13

14

17

15

16

14 Astronauts float in the cabin of the Space Shuttle Orbiter *Challenger* in this scene from the IMAX film, *The Dream Is Alive*. **15** An engineering model of the Voyager planetary probe: two probes were launched in March and July 1979, respectively, to explore the outer reaches of the solar system including the planets Jupiter, Saturn, Uranus, and Neptune. **16** The Pioneer 10 planetary probe was launched on March 3, 1972, and encountered the planet Jupiter late in December of 1973, transmitting valuable data back to Earth. The probe has since left the solar system. **17** The giant gas planet Jupiter, largest planet in the solar system, as photographed by the Voyager planetary probe.

18 The missile pit in the floor of the Space Hall allows taller rockets and missiles, like the Jupiter C, Scout D, and Minuteman 3, to be exhibited in the museum. **19** Cutaway of the RL-10 upper stage engine, the first hydrogen-oxygen engine operated in space. **20** The Tracking and Data Relay Satellite (TDRS) provides a link between Earth stations and space-

18

19

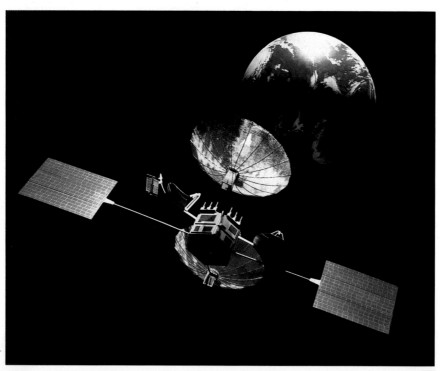

20

craft in flight. **21** This mockup of a Jules Verne projectile chamber is based on descriptions in his nineteenth-century novels, *From the Earth to the Moon* and *Around the Moon*. **22** The Geostationary Operation Environmental Satellite (GOES) provides daily coverage of weather developments on the Earth.

22

PAUL E. GARBER FACILITY

The full name of this mecca for aviation buffs in Suitland, Maryland, is the Paul E. Garber Preservation, Restoration, and Storage Facility. Dr. Garber joined the Smithsonian in 1920 and devoted his career to the acquisition and care of all types of aircraft. The unmatched collection he amassed led to the establishment of the original national air museum and subsequently The National Air and Space Museum. The Garber facility was dedicated to him on his eightieth birthday in 1979.

Although the facility has served since the fifties as a preservation, restoration, and storage center, some of its buildings were opened to the public in 1977. Of the two hundred aircraft housed here, about one hundred are on display and can be seen by appointment. The guided tour also includes a behind-the-scenes look at restorations in progress.

Preceding page: A 1912 Benoist-Korn Tractor biplane after restoration by the skilled technicians at the Garber Facility. **Inset:** The Benoist-Korn Tractor before restoration.

1 The Northrop N1M Flying Wing, first of the Northrop line of flying wings that led to the Northrop B-2 Stealth bomber, after restoration. **2** The Northrop N1M Flying Wing before restoration. **3** A Vought F4U-1D Corsair as it was delivered to the Garber Facility. **4** The Vought OS2U-3 Kingfisher after it was restored.

1

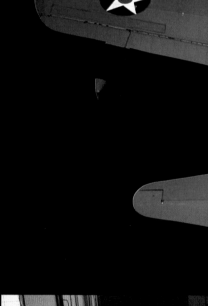

2

3

The Kingfisher was carried on battleships and cruisers and launched by catapult. **5** The woodworking skills of the Garber restoration technicians are clearly evident in this view of the Ecker Flying Boat before the fabric covering was applied.

Overleaf: The Manned Maneuvering Unit allows an astronaut to move about in space free of the spacecraft.

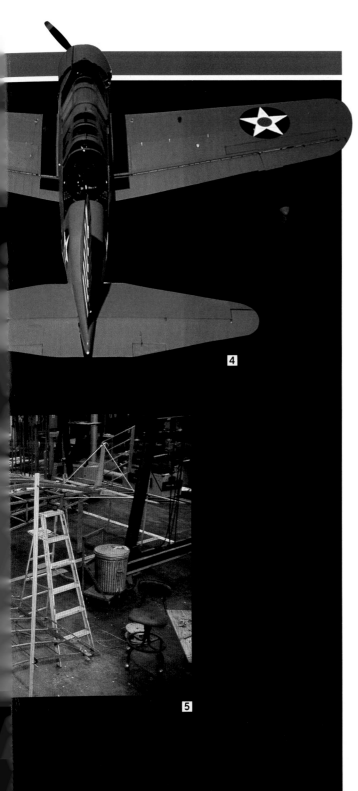

4

5

Credits

Except as noted below or in individual captions, all illustrations are courtesy of the National Air and Space Museum, Smithsonian Institution.

Page 1	IMAX film *On the Wing* (© Smithsonian Institution and Johnson Wax)
Pages 4–5	National Aeronautics and Space Administration photo
Pages 6–7	*Last Flight Home* by Robert Taylor, courtesy of The Military Gallery, Bath, England
Page 8	United States Air Force photo
Page 36, [7]	*Limitless Horizons* by Robert Taylor, courtesy of The Military Gallery, Bath, England
Page 43, [11]	*Into the Teeth of the Tiger* by William S. Phillips, courtesy of The Greenwich Workshop, Trumball, Connecticut
Page 49, [11]	*Hunters of Wadi Rum* by William S. Phillips, courtesy of the artist
Page 54, [9]	IMAX film *The Dream Is Alive* (© Smithsonian Institution and Lockheed Corporation)
Page 54, [10]	IMAX film *The Dream Is Alive* (© Smithsonian Institution and Lockheed Corporation)
Page 55, [11]	IMAX film *The Dream Is Alive* (© Smithsonian Institution and Lockheed Corporation)
Page 56, [14]	IMAX film *The Dream Is Alive* (© Smithsonian Institution and Lockheed Corporation)
Page 57, [17]	National Aeronautics and Space Administration photo
Page 64	National Aeronautics and Space Administration photo

Produced by the Book Development division of Smithsonian Institution Press.
Designed by Bob Crozier & Associates.

Library of Congress Cataloging-in-Publication Data

Lopez, Donald S., 1923–
The National Air and Space Museum : a visit in pictures / Donald S. Lopez.
    p.   cm.
ISBN 0-87474-710-4 :
1. National Air and Space Museum—Pictorial works.   I. Title.
TL506.U6W374 1989
629.1′074′0153—dc19   88-36586
                                    CIP